ABOUT THE BOOK

In the last few decades astronomers have made amazing discoveries about our universe. Some of these discoveries challenge our long-accepted laws of nature.

Among the most startling discoveries are quasars, pulsars, and black holes in space. Quasars, as big as stars but 1,000 billion times as bright, seem to exist at the very limit of our universe. Stars, called pulsars, give off radio signals so exact that astronomers thought they were being sent by intelligent beings from outer space. Possibly the most amazing discovery, though, is of black holes . . . tiny points in space so powerful that they can draw in and completely destroy objects or light that passes nearby.

Melvin Berger explores the theories concerning these discoveries. He examines the new and improved tools which enable astronomers to explore deeper into space, and he looks at what these discoveries are telling us about the world in which we live.

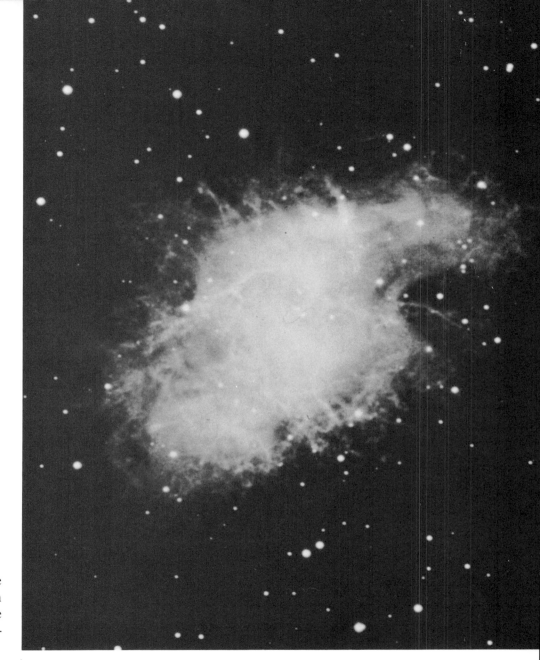

The Crab Nebula, where a supernova exploded on July 4, 1054, and where the first pulsar was discovered.

QUASARS, PULSARS
AND
BLACK HOLES IN SPACE

by Melvin Berger

G. P. Putnam's Sons, New York

PHOTOGRAPHS ARE COURTESY OF

Bell Telephone Laboratories: page 19.
Cornell University: page 22.
Hale Observatories: pages 8, 11, 15, 16, 24, 31, 32, 38, 41, 42, 51.
National Radio Astronomy Observatory: pages 20, 21, 26, 27.
Yerkes Observatory: page 14.
Cover and Frontispiece © California Institute of Technology and Carnegie Institute of Washington. Reproduced by permission from the Hale Observatories.

LIBRARY OF CONGRESS CATALOGING
IN PUBLICATION DATA

Berger, Melvin. Quasars, pulsars & black holes in space. Includes index. SUMMARY: Explores theories concerning three amazing astronomical discoveries of modern times. 1. Quasars—Juvenile literature. 2. Pulsars—Juvenile literature. 3. Black holes—Juvenile literature. 4. Cosmology—Juvenile literature. [1. Quasars. 2. Pulsars. 3. Black holes. 4. Cosmology] I. Title.
QB860.B47   523   76-50057
ISBN 0-399-20562-4   ISBN 0-399-61051-0 lib. bdg.

Designed by Aileen Friedman

CONTENTS

QUASARS, PULSARS
AND
BLACK HOLES IN SPACE

There are so many billions of stars in space that they form "clouds" of stars.

1

WONDERS IN THE SKY

The sky is a place of wonder and awe. It is filled with some of the most amazing objects known to man.

There is the sun, a swirling, glowing ball of gas larger than a million earths.

There are the other stars, some many times larger than the sun and much, much brighter.

There is our galaxy, a group of 100 billion stars that stretch out over trillions and trillions of miles in space.

And there are so many other galaxies that it is impossible to count them all.

These objects are truly amazing.

But there are also objects in the sky that are the size of stars and yet as bright as a thousand galaxies. These small, powerful sources of light are called quasars. One astronomer says that a quasar is like a flashlight with a beam as bright as all the lights in the city of Los Angeles.

Astronomers found the first quasar in 1960. By now they know of about 300 quasars. They believe that most of these are near the outer edge of the universe. As they learn more about quasars, they learn more about the size and shape of the universe.

There are other objects in space that "beep" regularly. These beeps are short bursts of radio waves. When these radio signals were first heard on earth, some people believed that living beings in space were sending messages. Some astronomers called the signals LGMs, for Little Green Men. Later, astronomers found that the radio signals were coming from rapidly spinning, pulsating stars. They named these stars pulsars.

Since 1967 about 150 pulsars have been found. No one is exactly sure how and why pulsars send out their signals. Most agree, though, that pulsars are left over from stars that exploded long ago. Some brilliant scientific detective work traced one of the pulsars back to a star that Chinese astronomers saw explode in the year 1054.

Finally, there are black holes. In 1972 astronomers found a spot in the sky where an immense star had collapsed into a ball a few miles wide. All the matter that was in the giant star is now squeezed into this ball. Because the ball has so much tightly packed mass, the pull of gravity is tremendous. It is so powerful that nothing, neither matter nor light nor heat, can escape from its surface. Anything that passes nearby is sucked in and disappears into the dark, invisible body that we call a black hole in space.

Some astronomers believe that there may be one billion black holes in our galaxy alone. Perhaps 90 percent of the whole universe is made up of these black holes. Some even say that black holes may be the source of all cosmic energy.

Even though quasars, pulsars, and black holes are billions of miles out in space, scientists already know a great deal

A galaxy is a group of 100 billion stars that stretches out over trillions and trillions of miles in space.

about them. But there are still many questions the scientists are trying to answer. Among them are: What is the source of the quasars' great energy? What causes the pulsars' beeps? What happens to matter inside the black hole?

Quasars are the most distant objects in the universe. As scientists study the quasars, they are learning more about how the universe began, how large it is, and how it is changing. Pulsars are very powerful sources of energy. Black holes destroy all nearby energy and matter. As scientists study pulsars and black holes they are gaining new understanding about energy and matter.

Nearly 500 years ago Copernicus discovered that the sun, and not the earth, is the center of the solar system. There was a major change in mankind's most basic ideas and beliefs. New discoveries about quasars, pulsars, and black holes in space may change our views even more.

2

TELESCOPES
EYES AND EARS TO THE SKY

People have always looked up at the sky with great curiosity. They saw the sun, the moon, and the planets of our solar system. They saw the points of light from the stars in our galaxy, the Milky Way. They tried to understand these strange objects in the sky as best they could.

OPTICAL TELESCOPES

With the invention of the optical telescope, in about 1609, astronomers were able to see much better and much farther than ever before. They could make out many details of the solar system that had been invisible. They were able to see stars that were too dim to see with the eyes alone.

The telescope is really a simple instrument. It brings the light from distant objects, such as the planets or the stars, to a point, or focus. This makes the image appear much larger than it does to the naked eye.

QUASARS, PULSARS
AND
BLACK HOLES IN SPACE

The world's largest refracting telescope is the one at Yerkes Observatory, Williams Bay, Wisconsin.

Light can be brought to a focus in two ways. The light can pass through a special glass lens that bends, or refracts, the light to a focus. Telescopes that work in this way are called refracting telescopes. The largest refracting telescope has a lens with a 102-centimeter (40-inch) diameter. It is at the Yerkes Observatory, at Williams Bay, Wisconsin.

The other way to bring light to a focus is to have it fall on a mirror that is slightly curved, so that the light is reflected to a single point. The largest reflecting telescope has a mirror with a diameter of 5.08 meters (200 inches). It is the Hale telescope, on Mount Palomar, in California.

With the large telescopes astronomers can study closely the planets in the solar system. They can study the nearby stars in our galaxy. And they can study other galaxies in the universe, each of them containing hundreds of billions of stars.

The arrow points to the most distant galaxy ever seen. It is 6 billion light years away.

QUASARS, PULSARS
AND
BLACK HOLES IN SPACE

Looking down the Hale telescope at the 5.08 meter reflecting mirror. Notice the astronomer seated at the focus point of the telescope.

In mid-1974 astronomers found the most distant galaxy ever seen. It is about 36 billion trillion miles out in space. The distance may be written as 36,000,000,000,000,000,000,000 miles.

Most astronomers prefer to express such large distances in light years. A light year is the distance that light, traveling at a speed of 186,000 miles per second, will cover in one year. A light year is about 6 trillion miles. To change light years into miles, you multiply the number of light years by 6 trillion. The distance to the farthest galaxy, then, is usually written as 6 billion light years.

RADIO TELESCOPES

The refractor and reflector telescopes can only be used at night, when the strong light from the sun does not hide the light from other stars. And they can only see far into the vastness of the universe on a few dozen nights a year when the weather is clear. On most nights the earth's atmosphere blocks and distorts the view, making it difficult to sight the dim, distant stars.

In 1931 a young radio engineer, Karl Jansky, accidentally discovered a completely new way to explore the vastness of the universe. Jansky was working at the Bell Telephone laboratories in Holmdel, New Jersey. His job was to learn more about the static that was interfering with trans-Atlantic and ship-to-shore radio communications.

To track down the cause of the static, Jansky built a giant radio antenna. On a wooden platform 100 feet long and 10 feet wide he constructed an antenna that looked like eight brass-frame doorways to nowhere. He mounted the antenna on four wheels from a junked Model T Ford and placed it on a round track so it could be turned to face in any direction. He nicknamed it the Merry-Go-Round.

Jansky heard a good deal of static through the earphones he had attached to the antenna. Most of it he knew was static from man-made sources and from electrical storms. But there was another kind of static, which he did not recognize. He described it as "very weak, very steady, causing a hiss in the phones."

For some time Jansky could not pinpoint the source of the "hiss." The difficulty was that the source was moving. Its path was related to the path of the sun. It rose in the east and set in the west. But each day it moved about four minutes ahead of the sun.

Finally Jansky was able to identify the hiss. It was coming from objects in our galaxy, far beyond our solar system. These objects were emitting radio waves. And it was the radio waves that were causing the hiss.

With Jansky's discovery came a new way of exploring the sky. Until then, all our knowledge of the sky came to us because the sun and stars emit light. Jansky's discovery showed that we could learn even more from radio waves emitted by objects in space.

Light waves and radio waves are both forms of energy. They come out, or radiate, from stars and from other sources in space. Astronomers measure both light and radio waves by their lengths, which are the distances from the crest of one wave to the next.

Light waves are much shorter than radio waves. They are measured in millionths of a meter, from crest to crest. The different colors of light depend on the exact length of the waves. The shortest waves are blue. The longer ones are green, yellow, and orange. The longest light waves are red in color.

Radio waves are about one million times longer than light waves. They range from less than a meter up to several hundred meters. The shortest radio waves are those used for ultrahigh-frequency television. The longer waves are for ordinary television and FM radio. The longest radio waves are used for AM radio.

Karl Jansky built his "merry-go-round" to find the source of the static that was interfering with trans-Atlantic radio communications.

Light waves are received and brought to a focus by the lens, or mirror, of an optical telescope. Radio waves are collected and brought to a focus by an antenna. The antenna works in the same way as the antenna of a television or radio set.

The antennas that pick up radio waves from outer space are called radio telescopes, even though they look nothing like optical telescopes. The science that studies these radio waves is called radio astronomy.

This solid-metal radio telescope has a diameter of 42.7 meters. The radio waves are brought to a focus at the receiver above the surface of the dish.

A typical radio telescope looks like an upturned dish or soup bowl. It is usually made of solid metal, or of open metal screening. Or it may consist of a row of antennas fixed in the ground. Sometimes these look like a line of dishes; others look like a series of television antennas.

The largest radio telescope in the world is set in a natural dishlike valley amongst the mountains near Arecibo, Puerto Rico. It has a diameter of 305 meters (1,000 feet). Its wire-mesh surface covers an area of about 20 acres. It is fixed to face one part of the sky. In Green Bank, West Virginia, is a 91.4 meter (300 foot) radio telescope. It is the largest steerable radio telescope and can be turned to face in any direction.

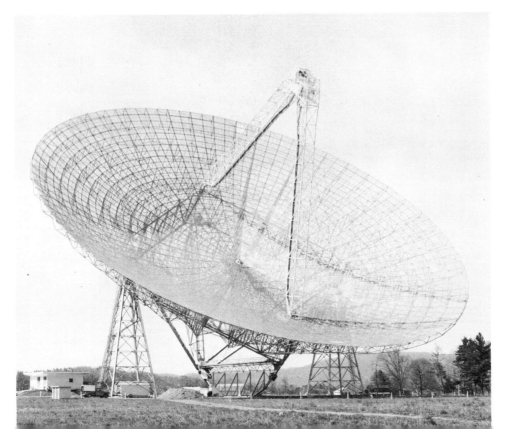

This wire-mesh radio telescope has a diameter of 91.4 meters. It is located at Green Bank, West Virginia.

The radio telescope near Arecibo, Puerto Rico, is the largest in the world. It has a diameter of 305 meters and covers an area of 20 acres.

By now radio telescopes have picked up some 3,000 sources of radio waves in space. They come from the sun and the moon, and from several planets in our solar system. They come from clouds of gas between the stars in our galaxy, and from stars that have exploded or are out of the ordinary in some way. But most radio waves come from beyond our galaxy. They come from other galaxies, millions or billions of light years away.

SPECTROSCOPES

Nowadays, astronomers seldom look through optical telescopes or listen to radio telescopes. Instead they use advanced tools and instruments that look and listen for them. Cameras make permanent records of what is seen through the optical telescope. Machines record the radio waves, which are received as curved lines, on long strips of graph paper. Computers and other electronic devices help the astronomers study and understand the data.

One of the most valuable instruments of modern astronomy is the spectroscope. The spectroscope is a device that is attached to the optical telescope. At the heart of the spectroscope is a glass prism, or a flat piece of glass with closely spaced lines scratched in the surface. The spectroscope spreads the light from the star into a full rainbow of colors—red, orange, yellow, green, blue, and violet.

Some stars produce a continuous band of color, or a spectrum, with one color blending into the next. Other stars produce bright up-and-down lines at various points in the spectrum. These lines are created by the chemical elements in the stars. Each element produces its own line or lines. By examining the lines, astronomers can identify the chemicals in the stars, as well as the temperature of the stars.

Astronomers know which chemicals they can expect to find in the stars. They know where the lines should be in the spectrum.

Over the years, the astronomers often noticed that the lines of the stars and galaxies were not where they should be. Some were moved over a bit toward the shorter wavelength, or blue, side of the spectrum. Others were shifted to the longer wave, or red, side.

Scientists assumed that the shifts were caused by the Doppler effect. The Doppler effect is the apparent shortening or lengthening of wavelength as the source of the waves moves toward or away from an observer. When stars are heading toward us, their lines are shifted toward the blue side of the spectrum. When stars are heading away, their lines are shifted toward the red side.

You have probably noticed the same Doppler effect on sound waves that astronomers noticed on light waves from the stars. Have you ever been in a fast-moving car when a car

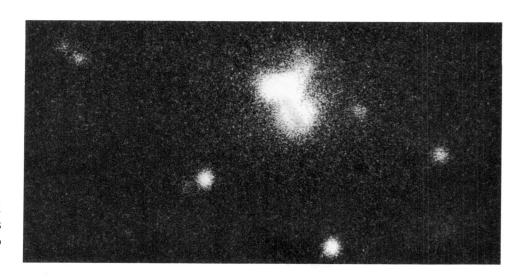

One of the most powerful radio sources is Cygnus A. It looks like two galaxies colliding.

going in the opposite direction passes you with its horn sounding? As the car approaches, you hear the pitch of the horn go up. Then, after it passes, you hear the pitch of the horn drop down again.

The pitch goes up as the car heads toward you because the sound waves become crowded together as the source of the sound moves closer. The pitch goes down as the car passes because the sound waves stretch out as you get farther apart.

The Doppler effect on light waves works the same way. If a source of light comes toward you, the light waves are squeezed together, and become shorter. The lines seen through a spectroscope move toward the blue, or short, side of the spectrum. If a source of light moves away, the waves spread out and become longer. The lines shift to the red, or long, side of the spectrum.

In studying the skies with the spectroscope, astronomers find that the lines of the nearby stars are either blue-shifted or red-shifted. According to the Doppler effect, this means that some nearby stars are heading toward us, and some are heading away. But almost all of the distant galaxies show red shifts. They are all moving away from us. By measuring the red shifts, astronomers can tell how fast the galaxies are moving and how far away they are. The red shift is a valuable way to locate objects in space.

ORBITING OBSERVATORIES

In the late 1940s and 1950s several rockets were sent up with equipment to detect X rays. X rays and other high energy beams are emitted by various objects in space. These rays and beams never reach the surface of the earth. The atmosphere

QUASARS, PULSARS
AND
BLACK HOLES IN SPACE

Blast off! With a burst of flame and a loud roar the rocket heads into space with equipment to observe the stars and galaxies from above the earth's atmosphere.

completely blocks out these emissions from objects in space. The only way for astronomers to study these X rays is to put an X-ray detector high above the earth's atmosphere.

In the 1960s and 1970s several artificial earth satellites were launched with even more advanced equipment. As they orbited the earth, they searched the sky for X-ray sources. The most successful of these satellites were—*Orbiting Astronomical Observatory Number Two*, in 1968; *Uhuru*, in 1970; and *Copernicus*, in 1973.

With these satellites astronomers have found about 160 sources of X rays. Some are clouds of gas, some are stars, and some are galaxies. In addition, there are a number of X-ray sources for which no visible object can be found.

The National Aeronautics and Space Administration now plans to launch a series of high-energy astronomical observatories, to carry on the search for other sources of energy in space.

High-energy astronomical observatories will provide astronomers with much more information about X-ray and other high-energy sources in space.

The optical and radio telescopes, the spectroscopes, and the orbiting observatories are increasing our knowledge of the universe. They are making possible some astonishing discoveries. And they are leading to a number of startling new ideas about our universe.

3

QUASARS

With optical telescopes, astronomers have located billions and billions of stars that emit light. With radio telescopes, astronomers have located 3,000 sources of radio waves. But until 1960, astronomers could not find a single star that emitted both light waves and radio waves.

NO ORDINARY STARS

Then, in 1960, astronomers Thomas Matthews and Allan Sandage turned the 5.08 meter Mount Palomar optical telescope toward a radio source in the sky known as 3C-48. The names of radio sources come from the catalogue of radio sources that was prepared by astronomers at Cambridge University, in England. The designation 3C means that the source appears in the third Cambridge catalogue; the number 48 means that this source is the forty-eighth item in the catalogue.

To the naked eye there is no visible light at the position of 3C-48. But a photograph taken with a long camera exposure showed a faint star at that very spot. Matthews and Sandage were thrilled to discover, at last, a star that gave off both light waves and radio waves. Their news made others want to look for stars that were emitting both light and radio waves.

Three years later, Maarten Schmidt used the 5.08-meter telescope to look at radio source 3C-273. The photograph he took through the telescope showed an ordinary star that looked a little like a fuzzy ball. But what was out of the ordinary was a taillike extension that came out of the star.

To study 3C-273 further, Schmidt passed its light through a spectroscope. Since it looked like a common star, he expected to see the lines of the chemical elements of common stars—hydrogen, helium, carbon, and oxygen. To his amazement, the lines formed an unusual pattern. They were unlike those produced by any other star he had ever seen. Could this star be made up of different chemical elements?

For a month Schmidt was baffled. The lines were not in their normal positions. Nor were they shifted a little to the red or a little to the blue side of the spectrum.

Then Schmidt had an idea. He decided to look for a really big shift. And that was indeed what he found.

All the usual lines were there. But they had moved a full 16 percent from their normal positions. They showed an immense shift to the red side of the spectrum.

The Doppler effect had caused the biggest red shift that had ever been seen. Since the greater the red shift the greater the speed, Schmidt was able to figure out that 3C-273 was

3C-48

3C-147

. 3C-273

3C-196

Here are four of the better-known quasars. They are among the most-distant objects in space. Note the tail extending from 3C-273.

hurtling away from the earth at a speed of 29,000 miles per second. Further calculations fixed the distance to 3C-273 at about one and a half billion light years. It was as far away as the most distant galaxies known at the time. In fact, this star-like body was at the very edge of the observed universe.

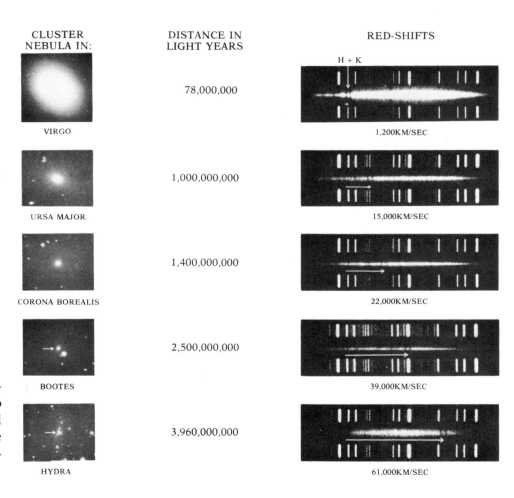

CLUSTER NEBULA IN:	DISTANCE IN LIGHT YEARS	RED-SHIFTS
VIRGO	78,000,000	H + K / 1,200KM/SEC
URSA MAJOR	1,000,000,000	15,000KM/SEC
CORONA BOREALIS	1,400,000,000	22,000KM/SEC
BOOTES	2,500,000,000	39,000KM/SEC
HYDRA	3,960,000,000	61,000KM/SEC

Each spectrum of a distant nebula shows two lines shifted to the red side. The greater the shift, the greater the distance to the nebula.

Other astronomers then went back to check the spectrum of 3C-48. This source had an even bigger red shift than 3C-273. The lines, as seen through the spectroscope, were moved 37 percent toward the red end of the spectrum. A shift of 37 percent means that this source is moving away from the earth at over 60,000 miles per second. Its distance from the earth was set at 3.6 billion light years.

The first stars found to be emitting both light and radio waves were 3C-48 and 3C-273. Their giant red shifts showed them to be moving outward at fantastic speeds. The red shifts also showed that they were among the most distant objects in space.

But most amazing of all, these stars were such powerful sources of energy that their light could be seen on Earth. At those distances, astronomers could barely see galaxies containing billions of brightly glowing stars. Yet here were single stars giving off as much light as 1,000 galaxies.

What were these strange, mysterious objects in space?

At first, astronomers called them quasi-stellar objects, which means "somewhat starlike" objects. But physicist Hong-Yee Chin shortened the name to "quasars," the name we use today for these amazing sources of energy in space.

So far about 300 quasars have been found. Perhaps the most astounding one is OQ-172 (item number 172 in the Ohio University catalogue of quasars). Discovered in 1973, OQ-172 shows an unheard-of red shift of 353 percent.

According to the astronomers' calculations, this quasar is speeding away from the earth at the incredible speed of 167,000 miles per second. This is nearly the speed of light, which is 186,000 miles per second. And, according to Einstein's theory of relativity, nothing in our universe can travel faster than the speed of light. The figures show that quasar OQ-172 is about 11 billion light years away.

Any object that is 11 billion light years distant is near the edge or boundary of the universe. The universe is the total space in which all matter is found. On the basis of their observations and calculations, most astronomers now believe that the universe extends some 13 billion light years in space. Quasars such as OQ-172, therefore, are the most distant objects in the universe.

MOST POWERFUL LIGHT IN THE UNIVERSE

There is little doubt that quasars are distant, fast-moving, powerful sources of energy. But now astronomers are asking: Where do the quasars get all of their energy? Where do they come from?

There are no final answers yet. But different groups of astronomers have come up with several interesting theories.

Perhaps each quasar is a giant mass of gas containing as much matter as 1,000 suns. The mass is so great that gravity forces it to collapse on itself. It is constantly drawing itself into a smaller and smaller volume. It might be the powerful force of the collapse of the gas that creates the great energy of the quasar.

Or maybe quasars are the meeting in space between matter and antimatter. Matter consists of normal atomic particles. Antimatter consists of identical atomic particles but with opposite charges. In experiments on earth, scientists have brought matter and antimatter together. This results in an explosion. Both the matter and the antimatter disappear, and a tremendous amount of energy is released. Quasars, then, could be collisions in space between matter and antimatter, and the energy could be coming from the force of the explosion.

Perhaps each quasar is the birth of a new galaxy. It might be a tightly packed collection of billions of very small, very bright, newly formed stars. This could explain the brightness of the quasar. Later, the stars will spread out and form an ordinary galaxy.

Or maybe quasars are old, dying galaxies. At the center of the galaxy the stars are very close together. There are many collisions between stars. Sometimes the stars come together and form even larger stars. Other times they collide and explode. Either way, great amounts of energy can be released. From the earth they would look like quasars.

Other astronomers do not accept any of these explanations. They say that the best way to understand quasars is to find another possible cause for the big red shifts.

Could it be gravity, and not the Doppler effect, that causes the red shift? If the gravity of a body is very powerful, it might hold back the light waves. This would make the light waves appear longer and therefore shifted to the red side of the spectrum.

In 1975 several scientists at the University of California's Lick Observatory studied the red shifts of quasar 3C-48 and of the surrounding cloud of dust. If gravity was indeed causing the red shift, they should find more red shift in the light from 3C-48 than in the light from the cloud.

They found the opposite. They are not sure why. But they do believe that their findings show that the red shift is not caused by gravity.

In the short time that we have known about quasars we have learned:

    —that they are numerous—over 300 have already been discovered

    —that they are moving fast away from the earth—at speeds up to 167,000 miles per second

    —that they are the most powerful sources of light in the universe—equal to trillions of stars

About these mysterious objects in space we still have to learn:

    —how they were created

    —the source of their energy

    —what causes their red shifts

    —what they can tell us about the size, shape, birth, and death of our universe

4

PULSARS

Everyone knows that stars twinkle. But not everyone knows that radio sources also "twinkle." In 1967 a group of radio astronomers at Cambridge University found out why.

RADIO SOURCES TWINKLE

Stars twinkle because we look at them through the earth's atmosphere. As the light waves bump into the molecules that make up the air and dust of the atmosphere, the light appears to waver, to go on and off.

Radio waves twinkle, as well. They twinkle because they pass by the sun on their way to the earth. Flying out from the sun is the solar wind. The solar wind is made up of atomic particles, mostly protons and electrons. It is the force of the solar wind that makes comets' tails always face away from the sun. Radio waves bump into the atomic particles of the solar

Do you know that comets' tails always face away from the sun? This photo clearly shows the head and tail of the famous Halley's comet.

wind as they head toward the earth. The collisons cause changes in the radio waves, making them appear to twinkle.

One day in August, 1967, Jocelyn Bell, a young member of the Cambridge group, was studying the charts of radio signals made the night before. She noticed that some radio waves picked up around midnight had gone on and off very rapidly. Since the earth is between the sun and the radio source at midnight, it could not have been the solar wind. What, then, could be causing the on-off signal?

Could it be some natural or man-made electrical activity on earth? You know how a thunderstorm or a large electrical appliance will cause static in a radio or television receiver. Bell and the other Cambridge astronomers checked out all possible interference from earth sources. None could explain the regular on-off radio signals from space.

Could the signals be messages from intelligent beings in space? The half-joking, half-serious search for little green men began. But the scientists could find no way that the signal could carry a message. And the energy was too strong to be coming from such a source. It had to come from a natural source. Also, the movement of the signal through the sky was related to the movement of a star, not to the movement of a planet.

The Cambridge team named the on-off radio source a pulsar, short for pulsating radio star. The particular pulsar that Jocelyn Bell discovered was called CP-1919. The CP means that it appears in the Cambridge catalogue of pulsars; the 1919 refers to its location in the sky.

Astronomers began a careful study of CP-1919. They found the period of time between one pulse and the next was exactly 1.33730113 seconds. Each pulse lasted exactly the same length of time—about 16/1,000ths of a second. The pulses were extremely regular, more regular than the ticks on any clock on earth.

THE GUEST STAR

Astronomers have already found about 150 pulsars in our galaxy and out in space. The rate of the pulses ranges from about 1/30th of a second to every 5 seconds. But they found only one pulsar that can be detected with an optical telescope, as well as with a radio telescope. This pulsar is in the Crab Nebula. It has become one of the best-known and most-studied objects in the heavens.

The pulsar in the Crab Nebula was first noticed by Chinese astronomers on July 4, 1054. They wrote that a "guest star" suddenly appeared in the sky. It was so bright that it could be seen by day. The only brighter object in the sky was the sun.

This star was not a new star. Rather it was an old star that had used up all of its fuel. The result was a powerful explosion with a tremendous release of light. Such a powerful explosion is called a supernova.

The force of the explosion sent a giant cloud of gas and particles hurtling out from the star. Eight hundred years later, when the English Earl of Rosse turned his 72-inch reflector telescope to the spot, he saw a cloudlike patch of light that reminded him of the legs and claws of a crab. He named it the Crab Nebula ("nebula" from the Latin word for "cloud").

Astronomers guess that only one or two supernova explosions occur every hundred years. Only large stars, those that are between one and a half and three times the size of the sun, explode this way. To understand supernovas and pulsars, we must look at the tiny atoms that make up these huge stars.

Ordinary stars, like the sun, are made of ordinary atoms. They consist of a central nucleus containing protons (with a plus charge) and neutrons (with no charge). Circling the nucleus, and at great distances from it, are electrons (with a minus charge). Most of the atom is empty space. A cubic inch of material from the sun weighs about two pounds.

After billions and billions of years, ordinary stars use up their fuel and begin to die. The electrons are stripped away from their atoms, until they consist only of nuclei. They shrink in size as the nuclei become packed more closely together than the atoms in an ordinary star. An old, dying star is called a white dwarf.

The sun is such an ordinary star. It now has a diameter of 864,000 miles. When it dies, it will become a white dwarf. It will probably have a diameter of about 6,000 miles. A cubic inch of the tightly packed material from a white dwarf weighs about 10 tons.

When a huge star, such as the supernova in the Crab

A supernova explosion makes a star about a million times brighter than it was before. The left photograph was taken in 1959. The photograph on the right was taken of the same sky area in 1972, and shows the appearance of a supernova.

QUASARS, PULSARS
AND
BLACK HOLES IN SPACE

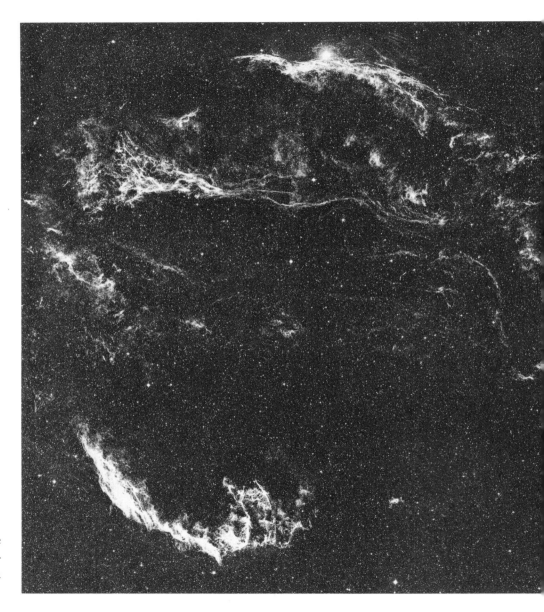

These wisps of clouds are
all that is left of a supernova that exploded far in
the past.

Nebula, explodes, it sends material out into space. The explosion also crushes and collapses the central core of the exploding star. The original star has a diameter of over one million miles. After the explosion, all the mass of that giant star is squeezed into a ball with a diameter of about ten miles!

The explosion also changes the atomic structure of the star. It forces the electrons into the nuclei of the atoms. Inside the nucleus, the electrons (minus charge) combine with the protons (plus charge), to form neutrons (no charge). The result is a crushed star made up only of neutrons, or a neutron star. A cubic inch of the super-heavy material of a neutron star weighs about 100 million tons!

SPECIAL ENERGY OF PULSARS

The pulsar in the Crab Nebula is really a neutron star. Neutron stars have very powerful magnetic fields. The magnetic field of a neutron star is between ten and a thousand billion times that of an ordinary star. This powerful magnetic field spins around with the neutron star as the star itself spins around.

The neutrons on the surface of the neutron stars decay. They separate into protons and electrons, and leave the surface. Some electrons get close to the magnetic poles and the very strong magnetic field. The electrons are set into faster and faster movement along a spiral path that is shaped by the magnetism. This produces a special kind of energy called synchroton radiation.

The synchroton radiation is beamed in one direction only—along the magnetic pole. Every time the star rotates so that the pole faces the earth, a signal heads toward the earth. It is like the rotating light on top of the control tower at an airport. It is always giving off light. But you can only see it when it is turned toward you.

The astronomers' observations and the laws of science support this explanation of pulsars. Scientists can also predict the behavior of the pulsars. It has been shown, for example, that a young neutron star pulses faster than an older one. The pulsar in the Crab Nebula has the fastest pulse rate of any pulsar—every 33/1,000ths of a second. We know that it is just over 900 years old. It is the youngest known pulsar. All of the other pulsars have slower pulse rates—up to every 5 seconds. These pulsars are much older.

Scientists also expect the pulsar's rate to slow down gradually. Careful measurements with the radio telescope at Arecibo, Puerto Rico, show that the pulsar in the Crab Nebula is slowing down exactly 38 billionths of a second every day. This amount is very small, but modern astronomers are able to measure such small differences. And such measurements add to our understanding of what pulsars are, and of how they work.

From what scientists now know about pulsars, they can piece together the following life story: Each pulsar was originally a massive star, much larger than our sun. It collapsed and became a tiny, rapidly rotating neutron star. By synchroton radiation, it gives off energy that reaches us in the form of radio waves. Some pulsars, such as the one in the Crab Nebula, also emit light waves, X rays, and other high-energy waves. As the pulsar ages, it slows down and stops emitting energy. In time it burns itself out and becomes cinder or ash, a cold rock traveling through space.

5

BLACK HOLES IN SPACE

Quasars and pulsars are discoveries of modern astronomy that boggle the mind. But as exciting as they are, they seem almost ordinary when compared with black holes in space.

GREATEST GRAVITY

As most ordinary stars die, they shrink and become white dwarfs. Larger stars, with 1.5 to 3 times the mass of the sun, collapse and become 10-mile wide neutron stars and pulsars.

But what happens to stars of even greater mass? What happens to a dying star with, say, 10 or 20 times the mass of an ordinary star?

When such a massive star collapses, it creates a tremendous force of gravity. The force of gravity is so strong that the collapse goes on and on. It continues until the whole mass of the original star is squeezed into a tiny speck in space. This speck may be no more than a mile or so in diameter. It is known as a black hole.

So much mass is crowded into so little space that it creates a fantastic force of gravity. The gravity in a black hole is greater than anywhere else in the universe. It is so strong that nothing can escape from it. Neither matter nor energy can overcome the mighty pull of gravity in a black hole.

To escape the gravity of earth, a rocket must reach a speed of seven miles a second. To get away from larger planets, with

Some astronomers believe that there may be billions of black holes in space. As we look at the great clouds of gas in the sky, we may be looking at black holes without seeing them.

more powerful gravity, the rocket must go even faster. But to escape the super-powerful gravity of a black hole, a capsule must reach a speed greater than 186,000 miles per second, which is the speed of light.

However, Albert Einstein, in his theory of relativity, demonstrated that no object can go faster than the speed of light. According to the laws of nature, therefore, it would be impossible for anything to get out of a black hole.

Let us imagine that an astronaut lands on the surface of a black hole. Since no rocket can travel faster than 186,000 miles per second, the astronaut can never leave.

So he tries to fire a bullet to earth to let everyone know that he is on a black hole in space. Even the most powerful gun could not fire a bullet that would travel above 186,000 miles per second. Therefore, the bullet, too, could not escape the surface of the black hole.

The astronaut tries to signal us by shining a powerful light beam toward the earth. He aims radio and sound waves in our direction. But we see and hear nothing because the gravity of the black hole does not let the light, radio, or sound waves escape.

In truth, of course, nothing like this could ever happen. Any object, or any form of energy, that passes near a black hole is sucked right into the small disk. It completely disappears. All matter, all energy, is destroyed when it is drawn into the black hole.

INVISIBLE AND MYSTERIOUS OBJECTS

Astronomers have been able to prove the existence of black holes by observing their effect on nearby stars. The best example is a star known as Cygnus X-1. Through their optical telescopes, astronomers see it as an enormous blue star. Measurements of the path of the visible star show that every 5.6 days it rotates around an invisible companion star. From the way the visible star moves, astronomers guess that the companion star has a mass at least eight times that of the sun.

Studies made with the orbiting observatory satellite *Copernicus* show that the unseen star is giving off a shower of X rays. And the X-ray flow drops every 5.6 days, following the same pattern as Cygnus X-1. Scientists know that when gases and particles from a nearby star are funneled into the tiny disk of a black hole, they will collide and send out powerful X rays. Therefore, since the invisible star is emitting X rays, and since it affects the visible star like a star with eight times the mass of the sun, the invisible companion is thought to be a black hole. Astronomers are also studying a few other stars that behave as if they are also close to black holes in space.

As astronomers learn more about black holes, they are being led to a fascinating question: What happens to the matter that disappears into the black holes?

A basic law of nature states that matter can be neither created nor destroyed. It can be changed. But it cannot be made from nothing; nor can it be removed leaving nothing. Yet the matter drawn into a black hole disappears without a trace.

The latest thinking about what happens to matter in black holes sounds more like science fiction than science. Yet it ties in with thoughts on quasars and pulsars.

Many astronomers believe that the matter that enters a black hole passes through a tunnel. They call the tunnel a "worm hole." Here the matter is changed according to laws stated by Einstein in the theory of relativity: The matter is changed into energy.

The matter then returns as a so-called "white hole." A white hole is a small body in space that is radiating immense amounts of energy. A quasar, you recall, is defined as a small body that radiates immense amounts of energy. Could it be that quasars are really white holes, the end points of the black hole–worm hole connection?

Other astronomers believe that the worm hole leads to another universe, or to many other universes, completely separate from ours. They say that the changes that occur in matter, as it passes through the black hole and the worm hole, create a new and different universe. Many of today's scientists think that such universes do exist.

There are, however, a number of scientists who consider black holes a mystery that will never be solved. They say that no one can learn from the outside what happens inside a black hole. And no instrument or person can ever enter a black hole and leave again.

Whether we will learn more about black holes and other universes remains to be seen. But of this we can be sure: Black holes will constitute one of the most exciting fields of scientific study for many years to come.

6

COSMOLOGY
NEW VIEWS OF THE UNIVERSE

Modern optical telescopes, radio telescopes, spectroscopes, and orbiting observatories are valuable new tools with which to explore the universe. Recent advances in physics, including Einstein's theory of relativity, improve our understanding of the basic laws of nature. And the discoveries in the years since 1960—of quasars, pulsars, and black holes in space—further stretch our thinking.

Together, these tools, theories, and discoveries are advancing the science of cosmology. Cosmology is the study of the universe—how it was born; its content, shape, and organization; and how it is changing.

THE EXPANDING UNIVERSE

In the years from 1912 to 1925, astronomer Vesto M. Slipher, of the Lowell Observatory, in Flagstaff, Arizona, was doing research on the red shift. He used a spectroscope to study the spectra of 40 galaxies. He observed that the spectrum of every one of them was shifted to the red side. Since the red shift was a result of the Doppler effect, Slipher concluded that all the galaxies were moving away from the earth. His figures showed that they were moving away at very high speeds. The fastest

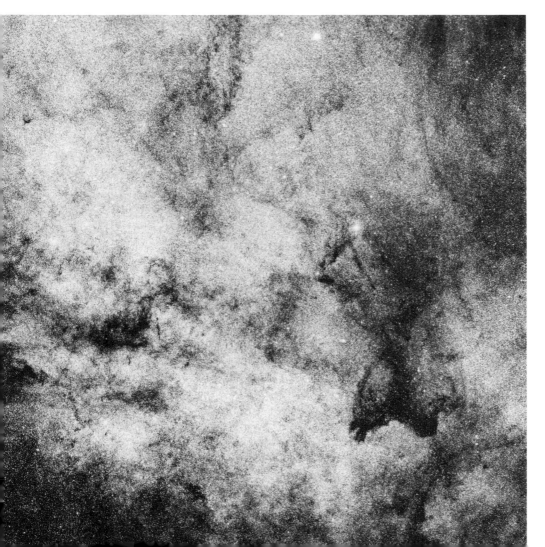

How did the universe begin? How is it changing? How will it end? These are the questions that cosmology is trying to answer.

one was traveling at over 1,000 miles per second.

Edwin Hubble's discoveries in the late 1920s carried Slipher's work a giant step forward. Working at the Mount Wilson Observatory, in California, he discovered a mathematical relationship between the speed of moving galaxies and their distance from earth: The farther away the galaxy, the faster it moves.

The speed of a galaxy is equal to its distance times a certain number, which is called the Hubble constant. Simply put, a galaxy travels 30 miles per second faster for every 3.25 million light years in distance. Thus, if a galaxy is 6.5 million light years away, it is moving at a speed of 60 miles per second.

Hubble also found that all the galaxies in our universe are moving away from us. But more than that, he realized that all galaxies are moving away from one another. They are spreading out, making our universe bigger and bigger. In other words, it is an expanding universe.

There is a certain distance, right now believed to be about 13 billion light years, to the farthest galaxies. And they continue to spread out into space, making the distances between them greater. There is no wall that marks the edge of the universe. Rather, the edge of the universe is composed of the most distant galaxies.

To better understand Hubble's findings, think of the universe as a loaf of raisin bread. The dough represents the space of the universe; the raisins represent the galaxies scattered about in space.

Before the bread is baked, the dough is compact; the raisins are relatively close together. As the bread bakes, it expands and grows larger. The raisins spread apart. All the raisins are not moving away from any one raisin. They are all moving away from one another. The dough (the universe) is expanding; the distance between the raisins (the galaxies) is becoming greater.

Now, suppose that after baking for an hour, our make-believe raisin bread becomes exactly twice as long, twice as wide, and twice as high as the original dough. As the bread expands during baking, the raisins move away from one another. During that hour, raisin A, which was originally 2 inches away from raisin B, moves 2 inches, to a total distance of 4 inches from raisin B. Raisin C, though, was originally 3 inches away from raisin B. It moves 3 inches, to a total distance of 6 inches from raisin B during the same period of time. What has happened is that the raisins have doubled their distance from each other because the loaf has doubled its size. If it had tripled its size, they would have tripled their distance from one another. But their speed is not constant. The closer the raisins are to one another originally, the slower they will move. Raisin A moves 2 inches per hour, while raisin B moves 3 inches per hour.

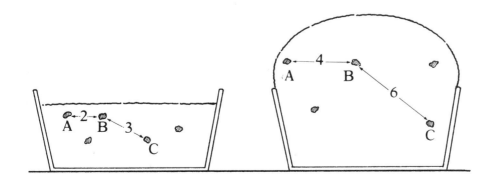

The expanding universe can be compared to raisin bread. At first the raisins are close together; when the bread is baked they spread apart. In the same way, the galaxies of the universe spread apart.

The way that raisins move in the dough as it grows in size is the same as Hubble's theory of how galaxies move in the expanding universe. The closer galaxies move away from one another more slowly than the distant ones. And the farther away the galaxy, the faster it is moving.

BIG BANG OR STEADY STATE?

The idea of an expanding universe was soon accepted by all astronomers. It explained many changes that were taking place in the universe. But the theory did not answer another basic question of cosmology: How did the universe begin?

One large group of astronomers hold what they call the big bang model of the universe.

According to the big bang model, there was a single moment when our universe was created. Before that, all of the matter that is now in the universe was crushed and squeezed into one big ball. (No one knows where this matter came from.) The matter in the ball, often called the primeval fireball, was under immense pressure, and at a temperature as high as 10 billion degrees.

Then came the explosion—the big bang. All the matter that was tightly packed in the primeval fireball was flung out into space. Every object in our universe—from the tiniest atomic particle to the largest galaxy—originated in that big bang.

There are a number of astronomers who do not accept this model of the origin of the universe. They believe instead in the steady-state model. According to this idea, the universe has always existed and has always been the same. There have always been the same number of galaxies, the number will stay the

same for all time to come, and the galaxies are evenly spread out in space, so that the universe looks the same from any point in space.

The steady-state believers accept the idea of an expanding universe. Therefore, they have to explain what fills the empty spaces created by the receding galaxies. They say that new galaxies are always being formed out of the clouds of dust and gas in space. In this way the average number of galaxies in all parts of the universe stays the same.

There is no direct way to test which model—the big bang or the steady state—is most accurate. Most astronomers, though, accept the big-bang model.

According to the big-bang theory, all the galaxies were created at one moment about 13 billion years ago. This photograph is an edge-on view of a galaxy, made up of billions of stars, that is far out in space.

The fact that the galaxies are moving farther and farther into space, astronomers say, could be the result of an explosion such as the big bang. Also, calculating back from the present speed and location of many galaxies, they find that all of the galaxies started out at the same time, about 13.3 billion years ago. Therefore, it is their belief that the big bang took place 13.3 billion years ago, the birth date of our universe.

Quasars are used as further evidence by the supporters of the big-bang theory. According to the steady-state model, quasars should be spread out evenly throughout the universe. But most quasars are found at great distances from earth. None is very close.

Then, too, the powerful light of a quasar, if we see it today, began its journey to the earth billions of years ago. Could the immense energy of the quasars that we see today really be the tail end of the big-bang explosion?

THE CHANGING UNIVERSE

In 1965 Arno A. Penzias and Robert W. Wilson, of the Bell Telephone Laboratories, picked up a strange radio signal on their sensitive radio telescope. Oddly enough, the signal seemed to be coming from all directions. No matter how they faced the radio telescope, they picked up the same signal. They studied it and tried to determine its source. They found that the signal came from an object that was radiating a temperature of 3 degrees above absolute zero.

According to the big-bang model, the explosion took place 13 billion years ago, at a temperature of 10 billion degrees. Since then, the material from that explosion has been losing its heat. Scientists calculate that the present temperature of these bodies should now be about 3 degrees above absolute zero. And this material should be scattered at great distances all around the edge of the universe. Could the signal that Penzias and Wilson detected be from the cooling embers of the original big bang?

Astronomers are excited by the triumphs and challenges of modern cosmology. In their observatories and at their desks they are trying to learn more, to understand better, and to find more positive proofs for their many theories.

They are hoping that quasars, pulsars, and black holes in space will help provide answers to some of their questions. Quasars are the oldest objects in the universe known to scientists. The light observable from a quasar started its trip to earth billions of years ago, soon after the big bang. As we study this light, we hope to learn more about events at that time.

Quasars are also the most distant objects we know of. They are trillions and trillions of miles out in space. As we observe them, we may be seeing the very edge of our universe.

The black holes have more energy than any other object in the universe. Gravity is stronger in black holes than anywhere else, and black holes are the most powerful sources of X rays. No one can even guess what secrets the black holes hold about the energy in our universe, and about the possible existence of universes other than our own.

Quasars, pulsars, and black holes are amazing objects in themselves. But they become still more amazing as they are used to unlock the most basic secrets of our universe.

GLOSSARY

ANTIMATTER Matter that is made up of atomic particles that are identical to ordinary particles, except that they have opposite charges. For example, the protons in ordinary matter have positive charges; the antiprotons in antimatter have negative charges.

ASTRONOMY The branch of science that studies the objects—such as planets, stars, galaxies, and clouds of dust and gas—as well as the energy and the forces, found throughout the universe.

ATOM The smallest part of an element that has all the characteristics of that element.

BIG BANG The theory, held by most astronomers, that the universe began with an immense explosion some 13 billion years ago.

BLACK HOLE The remains of the collapse of a giant star, whose powerful gravity captures all nearby matter and energy, allowing nothing to escape.

COMET   A small body of ice and dust in orbit around the sun. When a comet approaches the sun, it forms a bright tail that always faces away from the sun because of the pressure of the solar wind.

COSMOLOGY   The study of the origins, organization, and development of the universe.

DOPPLER EFFECT   A change in the wavelength of light or sound noted by an observer as the source moves toward or away from the observer.

ELECTRON   An atomic particle, with a negative charge, that revolves around the nucleus of an atom.

FOCUS   The point where light rays or radio waves come together.

GALAXY   An immense system containing billions of individual stars.

GRAVITY   The attraction of matter to matter. The greater the amount of matter in an object, the greater its pull of gravity.

HUBBLE CONSTANT   The number that expresses the relationship between the speeds of the galaxies and their distances from one another.

LIGHT YEAR   The distance that light travels in a vacuum in one year—approximately 6 trillion miles.

NEBULA   A cloud of dust or gas in space.

NEUTRON   An atomic particle, found within the nucleus, having no charge.

NEUTRON STAR   A small collapsed star made up entirely of neutrons.

NUCLEUS (OF AN ATOM)   The heavy central part of an atom, made up mostly of protons and neutrons. The electrons revolve around the nucleus.

PLANET   Any large, cold body in orbit around a central star.

PROTON An atomic particle found in the nucleus, along with the neutrons. The proton has a positive charge.

PULSAR A small source of pulsating radio waves, thought to be a neutron star.

OPTICAL TELESCOPE See TELESCOPE.

QUASAR A starlike object, extremely distant, that is a more powerful source of light than an entire galaxy.

RADIO ASTRONOMY The science based on observations made of radio waves from space.

RADIO TELESCOPE An antenna that collects radio waves from space, just as an optical telescope collects light waves from space.

RED SHIFT The movement of a wavelength of light toward the red side of the spectrum. This is produced by the Doppler effect when a body is moving away from an observer.

REFLECTING TELESCOPE An optical telescope in which the light rays are brought to a focus by reflection from a curved mirror.

REFRACTING TELESCOPE An optical telescope in which the light rays are brought to a focus by being bent, or refracted, by a glass lens.

SOLAR SYSTEM The sun, and the planets that revolve around the sun.

SOLAR WIND A steady flow of atomic particles from the sun.

SPECTROSCOPE A tool that separates light into a rainbowlike spectrum of colors.

SPECTRUM The separation of light into its different colors and wavelengths.

STAR An intensely hot sphere of gas, giving off heat, light, and other radiations.

STEADY STATE A theory that holds that the universe has no beginning or end, and that new matter is continually being created.

SUPERNOVA An explosion of a star, which increases the light from the star very suddenly and drastically.

SYNCHROTON RADIATION The radiation produced by charged particles moving at very high speeds in a powerful magnetic field.

TELESCOPE An optical instrument used to view and photograph objects in space. The telescope makes it possible to see some objects invisible to the naked eye, and adds details to objects only seen dimly by the eye. See REFLECTING TELESCOPE and REFRACTING TELESCOPE.

UNIVERSE The totality of all matter that exists, and the space that it occupies.

WHITE DWARF The collapsed state of an ordinary star that is dying because it has used up all of its fuel.

WHITE HOLE The opposite of a black hole: The return to our universe of the matter and energy that disappeared in a black hole.

WORM HOLE A connection between two universes, or between a black hole and a white hole.

X RAY A form of radiation similar to light, but with very short wavelengths.

INDEX

ABOUT THE AUTHOR

Melvin Berger is a graduate of the University of Rochester. He did graduate work at Teachers College, Columbia University, and the University of London in England. He has many years of experience as a public school teacher and has numerous scientific articles for magazine publication to his credit. He has written many science books for young readers, and six of these books have been given the Outstanding Science Books for Children Award of the National Science Teachers Association and the Children's Book Council.

37611

QUASARS, PULSARS AND BLACK
HOLES IN SPACE   5.29

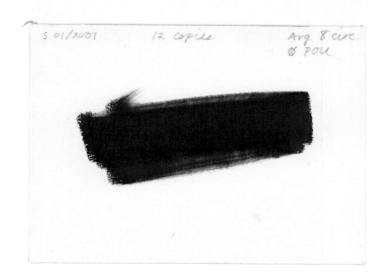

S 01/2001   12 copies   Avg 8 circ.
                                  Ø POU